Best Start

Telling the Time

PaRragon

Bath · New York · Cologne · Melbourne · Delhi
Hong Kong · Shenzhen · Singapore · Amsterdam

Helping your child

- The activities in this book should be enjoyed by your child. Try to find a quiet place to work.

- Your child does not need to complete each page in one go. Always stop before your child grows tired, and come back to the same page another time.

- Set aside time to do the activities together.

- There are parent notes at the bottom of the pages to help you support your child.

- Give lots of encouragement and praise.

- Use the stickers as rewards and incentives.

- The answers are on page 24.

This edition published by Parragon Books Ltd in 2014

Parragon Books Ltd
Chartist House
15–17 Trim Street
Bath BA1 1HA, UK
www.parragon.com

Copyright © Parragon Books Ltd 2006

Written by Betty Root
Consultant: Nina Filipek
Illustrated by Simon Abbot

ISBN 978-1-4723-4824-1

Printed in China

Contents

Clock Faces

Trace over the numbers on the clock face.
The short hand shows the hours.
The long hand shows the minutes.
The long hand moves faster.
The short hand moves slower.

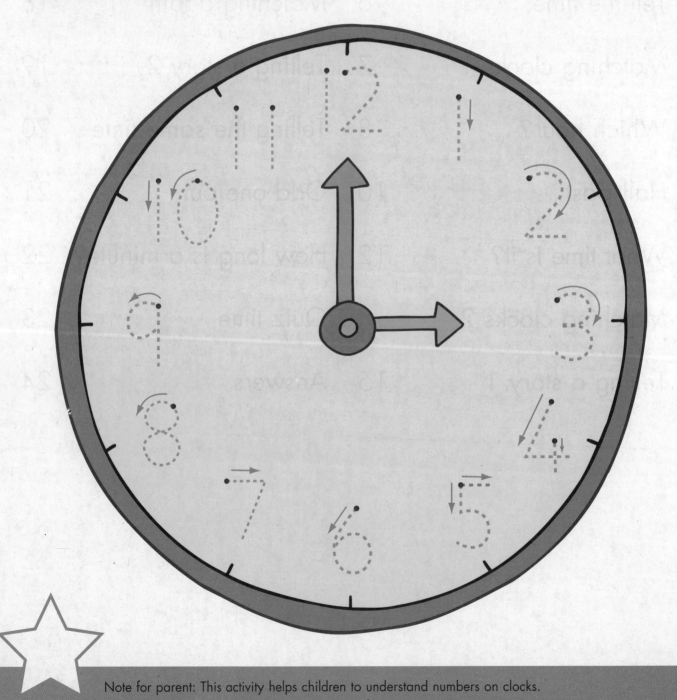

Note for parent: This activity helps children to understand numbers on clocks.

Which comes first?

Look at the two rows of pictures.
Put a ✓ by the one that comes first in each row.

Note for parent: Use words such as before, after, earlier, later when talking about
sequences of events.

5

Tell the time

Practise telling the time on these clock faces.
The big hand is on the 12. Which number is the
small hand pointing to? Write the number in each box.

1. ⬜ o'clock

2. ⬜ o'clock

3. ⬜ o'clock

4. ⬜ o'clock

5. ⬜ o'clock

6. ⬜ o'clock

Note for parent: This activity helps children to look carefully at the differences between the
long and short hands.

Matching clocks 1

Say what time it is on each clock.
Draw a line to join each clock to the correct time.
The first one has been done for you.

3:00

12:00

8:00

1:00

6:00

Which hour?

Look at each clock. Write the time in the box.

1.

[ ] o'clock

2.

[ ] o'clock

3.

[ ] o'clock

4.

[ ] o'clock

5.
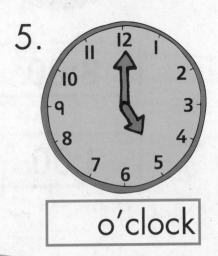

[ ] o'clock

6.

[ ] o'clock

Draw hands on each clock to show the right time.

5 o'clock

9 o'clock

3 o'clock

12 o'clock

2 o'clock

10 o'clock

Half past

When the long hand is on the 6 you say it is half past
the hour. The short hand will be between two numbers.
If the long hand is on the 6 and the short hand is
between 2 and 3 it is half past 2, which can also be
written as 2:30. Tell the time on these clocks.

Note for parent: This activity helps children to practise telling half-hourly time.

What time is it?

Morning time.
Draw the hands on these clocks.

At 7.30 I get up.

At 9 o'clock I eat breakfast.

At 10.30 I am at school.

At 11 o'clock I have a drink.

Note for parent: This activity helps children to tell the difference between morning and afternoon.

Afternoon time.
Draw the hands on the clocks.

At 5.30 I watch TV.

At 6 o'clock I eat my tea.

What time do you go to bed?
Draw the hands on this clock.

Matching clocks 2

Say what the time is on each clock. Draw lines to join the clocks that tell the same time.

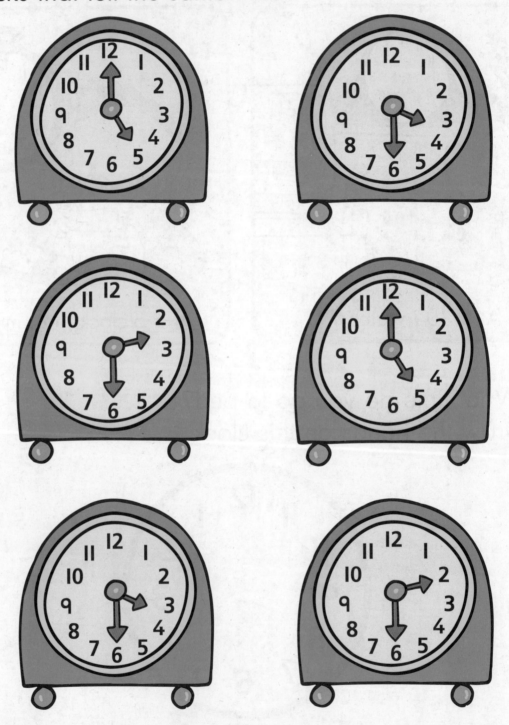

Note for parent: This activity helps children to look at clock faces carefully.

Telling a story 1

These pictures tell a story but they are in the wrong order. Write numbers in each box to put them in the correct order. Start with number 1.

Note for parent: Use words such as before, after, earlier, later when talking about sequences of events.

15

Quarter past

When the long hand is on 3, it is quarter past the hour. The short hand will be just past the number of the hour. Tell the time on these clocks and write the numbers in the boxes.

1. quarter past ☐

2. quarter past ☐

3. quarter past ☐

4. quarter past ☐

Note for parent: This activity introduces your child to quarter past.

Quarter to

When the long hand is on the 9, it is quarter to the hour. The short hand will be just before the number of the hour. Tell the time on these clocks and write the numbers in the boxes.

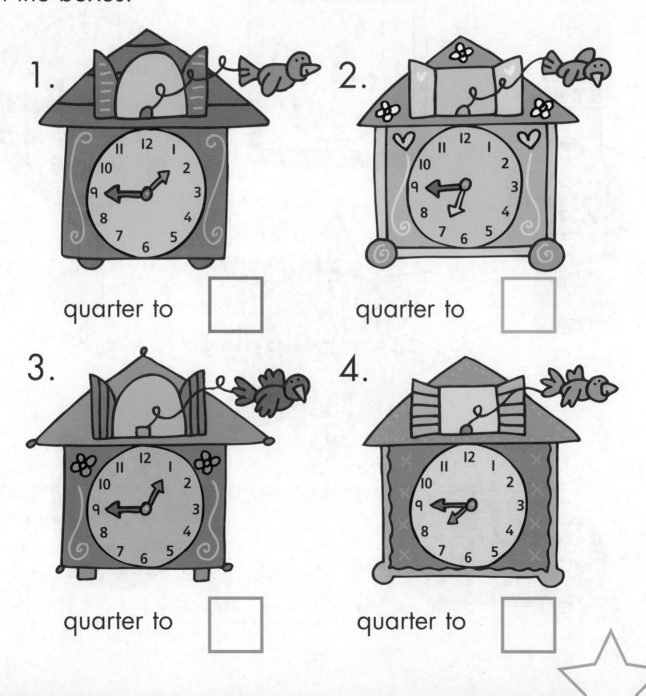

1. quarter to ☐

2. quarter to ☐

3. quarter to ☐

4. quarter to ☐

Note for parent: This activity introduces your child to quarter to.

17

Matching again

Say what the time is on each clock. Draw lines to join
the clocks that tell the same time.

Note for parent: This activity gives practice in telling the time using quarter past and quarter to.

Telling a story 2

These pictures tell a story but they are in the wrong order. Write numbers in each box to put them in the correct order. Start with number 1.

Note for parent: This activity gives more practice in talking about sequences of events.

19

Telling the same time

Look at the clocks in each box. Draw the hands or write the numbers to tell the same time.

3:15

12:30

:

2:30

:

14:30

The last one is difficult. Did you get it right?

20

Odd one out

Look at the clocks carefully. Cross out the one in each row that tells a different time.

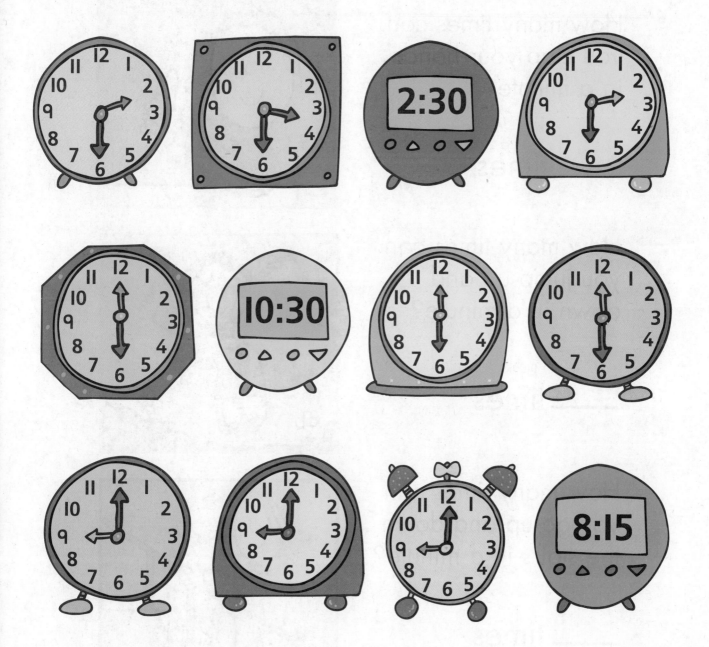

How long is a minute?

There are 60 seconds in a minute, and 60 minutes in an hour. An adult can help you time a minute.

How many times can you clap your hands in a minute?

_____ times

How many times can you jump up and down in a minute?

_____ times

How many times can you go up and down the stairs in a minute?

_____ times

Note for parent: This activity helps children to learn how long a minute is (a digital watch is useful to time a minute).

Quiz time

Write the correct time in each box.

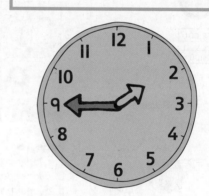

Answers

Page 5

Page 6

1. 1 o'clock
2. 10 o'clock
3. 6 o'clock
4. 7 o'clock
5. 9 o'clock
6. 11 o'clock

Page 7

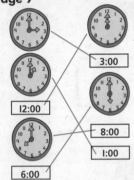

Page 8

1. 4 o'clock
2. 1 o'clock
3. 10 o'clock
4. 9 o'clock
5. 5 o'clock
6. 2 o'clock

Page 9

Pages 10 and 11

page 10 top: half past 4, half past 6;
bottom: half past 12, half past 1.
page 11 top: half past 8, half past 9;
bottom: half past 10, half past 11.

Page 12

Page 13

Page 14

Page 15

Page 16

1. quarter past 5
2. quarter past 11
3. quarter past 10
4. quarter past 6

Page 17

1. quarter to 2   2. quarter to 7
3. quarter to 1   4. quarter to 8

Page 18

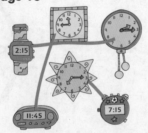

Page 19

Page 20

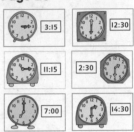

Page 21

Page 23

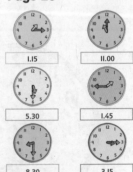

24